Workbook

Science

PEARSON
Scott
Foresman

Editorial Offices: Glenview, Illinois • Parsippany, New Jersey • New York, New York
Sales Offices: Needham, Massachusetts • Duluth, Georgia • Glenview, Illinois
Coppell, Texas • Sacramento, California • Mesa, Arizona

www.sfsuccessnet.com

Series Authors

Dr. Timothy Cooney
Professor of Earth Science and Science Education
University of Northern Iowa (UNI)
Cedar Falls, Iowa

Dr. Jim Cummins
Professor
Department of Curriculum, Teaching, and Learning
The University of Toronto
Toronto, Canada

Dr. James Flood
Distinguished Professor of Literacy and Language
School of Teacher Education
San Diego State University
San Diego, California

Barbara Kay Foots, M.Ed.
Science Education Consultant
Houston, Texas

Dr. M. Jenice Goldston
Associate Professor of Science Education
Department of Elementary Education Programs
University of Alabama
Tuscaloosa, Alabama

Dr. Shirley Gholston Key
Associate Professor of Science Education
Instruction and Curriculum Leadership Department College of Education
University of Memphis
Memphis, Tennessee

Dr. Diane Lapp
Distinguished Professor of Reading and Language Arts in Teacher Education
San Diego State University
San Diego, California

Sheryl A. Mercier
Classroom Teacher
Dunlap Elementary School
Dunlap, California

Dr. Karen L. Ostlund
UTeach, College of Natural Sciences
The University of Texas at Austin
Austin, Texas

Dr. Nancy Romance
Professor of Science Education & Principal Investigator
NSF/IERI Science IDEAS Project
Charles E. Schmidt College of Science
Florida Atlantic University
Boca Raton, Florida

Dr. William Tate
Chair and Professor of Education and Applied Statistics
Department of Education
Washington University
St. Louis, Missouri

Dr. Kathryn C. Thornton
Professor
School of Engineering and Applied Science
University of Virginia
Charlottesville, Virginia

Dr. Leon Ukens
Professor of Science Education
Department of Physics, Astronomy, and Geosciences
Towson University
Towson, Maryland

Steve Weinberg
Consultant
Connecticut Center for Advanced Technology
East Hartford, Connecticut

Consulting Author

Dr. Michael P. Klentschy
Superintendent
El Centro Elementary School District
El Centro, California

ISBN: 0-328-14586-6
ISBN: 0-328-20063-8

3 4 5 6 7 8 9 10 V084 13 12 11 10 09 08 07 06 05

Unit A
Life Science

Chapter 1 • Needs of Plants and Animals
How to Read Science 1
Lesson 1: Lesson Review 2
Lesson 2: Lesson Review 3
Lesson 3: Lesson Review 4
Lesson 4: Lesson Review 5
Lesson 5: Lesson Review 6
Lesson 6: Lesson Review 7
Take-Home Booklet 9

Chapter 2 • Growing and Changing
How to Read Science 11
Lesson 1: Lesson Review 12
Lesson 2: Lesson Review 13
Lesson 3: Lesson Review 14
Lesson 4: Lesson Review 15
Lesson 5: Lesson Review 16
Take-Home Booklet 17

Chapter 3 • Plants and Animals All Around
How to Read Science 19
Lesson 1: Lesson Review 20
Lesson 2: Lesson Review 21
Lesson 3: Lesson Review 22
Lesson 4: Lesson Review 23
Lesson 5: Lesson Review 24
Take-Home Booklet 25
Unit A Math in Science 27

Unit B
Earth Science

Chapter 4 • Our Land, Water, and Air
How to Read Science 28
Lesson 1: Lesson Review 29
Lesson 2: Lesson Review 30
Lesson 3: Lesson Review 31
Lesson 4: Lesson Review 32
Lesson 5: Lesson Review 33
Lesson 6: Lesson Review 34
Take-Home Booklet 35

Chapter 5 • Weather and Seasons
How to Read Science 37
Lesson 1: Lesson Review 38
Lesson 2: Lesson Review 39
Lesson 3: Lesson Review 40
Lesson 4: Lesson Review 41
Lesson 5: Lesson Review 42
Lesson 6: Lesson Review 43
Take-Home Booklet 45
Unit B Math in Science 47

Unit C
Physical Science

Chapter 6 • Matter
How to Read Science 48
Lesson 1: Lesson Review 49
Lesson 2: Lesson Review 50
Lesson 3: Lesson Review 51
Lesson 4: Lesson Review 52
Lesson 5: Lesson Review 53
Lesson 6: Lesson Review 54
Take-Home Booklet 55

Chapter 7 • Heat and Light
How to Read Science 57
Lesson 1: Lesson Review 58
Lesson 2: Lesson Review 59
Lesson 3: Lesson Review 60
Lesson 4: Lesson Review 61
Take-Home Booklet 63

Chapter 8 • How Things Move
How to Read Science 65
Lesson 1: Lesson Review 66
Lesson 2: Lesson Review 67
Lesson 3: Lesson Review 68
Lesson 4: Lesson Review 69
Lesson 5: Lesson Review 70
Lesson 6: Lesson Review 71
Take-Home Booklet 73
Unit C Math in Science 75

Unit D
Space and Technology

Chapter 9 • Day and Night Sky
How to Read Science 76
Lesson 1: Lesson Review 77
Lesson 2: Lesson Review 78
Lesson 3: Lesson Review 79
Lesson 4: Lesson Review 80
Take-Home Booklet 81

Chapter 10 • How Things Work
How to Read Science 83
Lesson 1: Lesson Review 84
Lesson 2: Lesson Review 85
Lesson 3: Lesson Review 86
Lesson 4: Lesson Review 87
Lesson 5: Lesson Review 88
Take-Home Booklet 89
Unit D Math in Science 91

Alike and Different

Find the two nonliving things in the left box.
Circle them.
Find the living thing in the right box.
Put an X on it.

Alike	Different

 Directions: Look at the pictures in the left box. Circle the two pictures that show nonliving things. Tell how the two things are alike. Look at the pictures in the right box. Put an X on the picture that shows a living thing. Tell how it is different from the other two things.
Home Activity: Find a picture in a magazine or newspaper. Ask your child to identify several nonliving things in the picture.

What are nonliving things?

Color each nonliving thing.

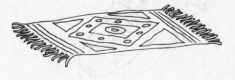

 Directions: Look at the three pictures in each row. Decide which picture shows something that is nonliving. Color that picture.
Home Activity: Look around a room in your home. Have your child tell which things in the room are nonliving.

© Pearson Education, Inc.

Name _____

What are living things?

Color the living things.

Directions: Look at the picture. Think about which things in the picture are living. Color each living thing.
Home Activity: Read a storybook to your child. Ask your child to identify several living things in the book.

How does air help plants and animals?

Put an X on the thing that does <u>not</u> need air to live.

Directions: Look at the two pictures in each row. Decide which picture shows something that does <u>not</u> need air to live. Put a large X on that picture.

Home Activity: Say each of the following pairs and ask your child to identify which thing needs air to live: fish/water; rock/tree; child/chair; dish/cat.

Name _____

How does water help plants and animals?

Draw something that needs water to live.

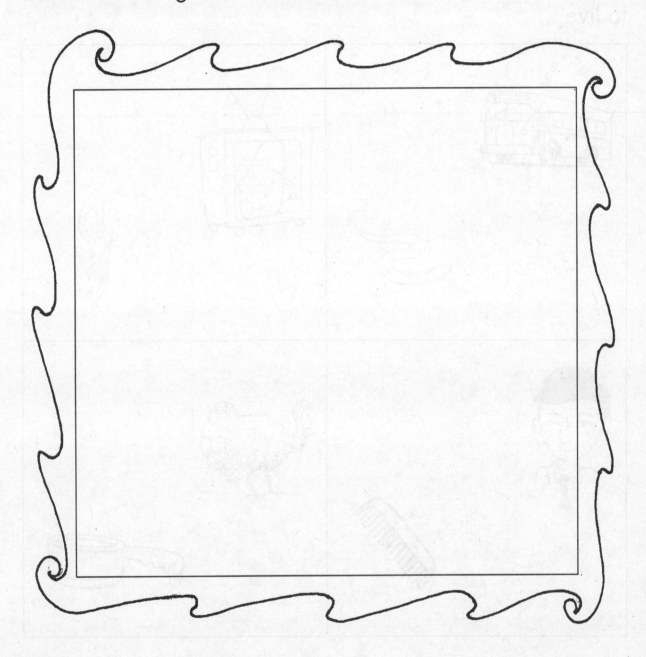

Directions: Think about things that need water to live. Choose one of the things and draw a picture of it in the box.

Home Activity: Using a magazine, newspaper, or book, point to pictures of living things and nonliving things and ask your child whether each thing needs water to live.

How does food help plants and animals?

Circle each thing that needs food and sunlight to live.

 Directions: Look at the two pictures in each box. Decide which picture shows something that needs food and sunlight to live. Circle that picture.

Home Activity: Write *desk, boy, wall, dog, flower,* and *fan* on index cards or scraps of paper. Help your child sort the things into those that need food and sunlight to live and those that do not.

What else do plants and animals need?

Color the things that need space or shelter to live.

 Directions: Look at the picture. Think about which things in the picture need space or shelter to live. Color those things.
Home Activity: Point to each thing your child colored on the page. Ask your child to tell why he or she colored that thing. Point to other things in the picture. Ask your child to tell why he or she did not color those things.

Notes

Dear Family,

In the science chapter Needs of Plants and Animals, your child is learning the differences between living and nonliving things. The class learned that plants and animals are living things. The class also learned that plants and animals have certain needs. The children also investigated how some nonliving things are made to look like living things.

While learning about living and nonliving things, the children also learned many new vocabulary words. Help your child to make these words a part of his or her own vocabulary by using them when you talk together about living and nonliving things.

nonliving	water
objects	animals
living	food
plants	light
need	space
air	shelter

The following pages include activities that you and your child can do together. By participating in your child's education, you will help to bring the learning home.

Family Science Activity

What Is Living in Your Home?

Steps

1. Walk from room to room with your child. You may also walk around outside to find more living things.
2. Ask your child to point out any living things.
3. Ask your child how he or she knows the things are living.
4. Encourage your child to draw a picture of one of the living things, including some of the needs of the thing he or she chose. For example, houseplants need sunlight, water, and air.
5. Display the picture in a central area.

Workbook

Look at the plants and animals below.

Color the things that both the plants and animals need.

Fun Fact

A camel's hump does not hold water at all. Its hump is made of fat. The camel uses this fat to live when it does not have enough food.

Living Things in a Living Room

Color the living things.
Circle the nonliving things.

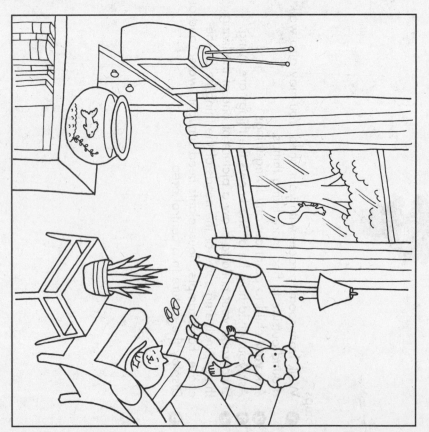

Alike and Different

Draw two animals that are alike in the left box.
Draw two animals that are different in the right box.
Tell how the animals are alike and different.

Alike	Different

Directions: In the left box, draw two animals that are alike in some way. Tell how the animals are alike. In the right box, draw two animals that are different in some way. Tell how the animals are different.
Home Activity: Show a picture of your child as a baby. Ask your child how he or she is both like and different from the baby.

Name _____

How do animals change?

Show how the animal grows.
Number the pictures in order.

_____

_____

_____

_____

Directions: Tell what you see in each picture. Decide what is the correct order for the pictures. Write 1, 2, 3, or 4 on the line under each picture.
Home Activity: On separate sheets of paper, draw simple sketches of a seed, a seedling, a plant with two leaves, and a plant with many leaves. Mix the pictures and let your child put them in the correct order.

Workbook

How do animals move?

Color the animals that move like the word says.

fly

crawl

run

swim

Directions: Name the animal at the beginning of the row and tell how that animal moves. Then find and color the animal in the row that moves in the same way.
Home Activity: Have your child pantomime each action named on the page. Together think of other animals that move in that way. Make a list of the animals for each action.

How are these animals alike and different?

Which two animals are alike in some way?
Circle their pictures.

 Directions: Name the animals in the row. Think about how two of the animals are alike. Do they run? Do they fly? Do they swim? Circle the two animals that are alike in some way.

Home Activity: Point to the tiger and the lion. Ask your child how these two animals are alike. Repeat the activity with the worm and the fish.

Name _____

What are the parts of a plant?

Draw lines to match the pictures and words.

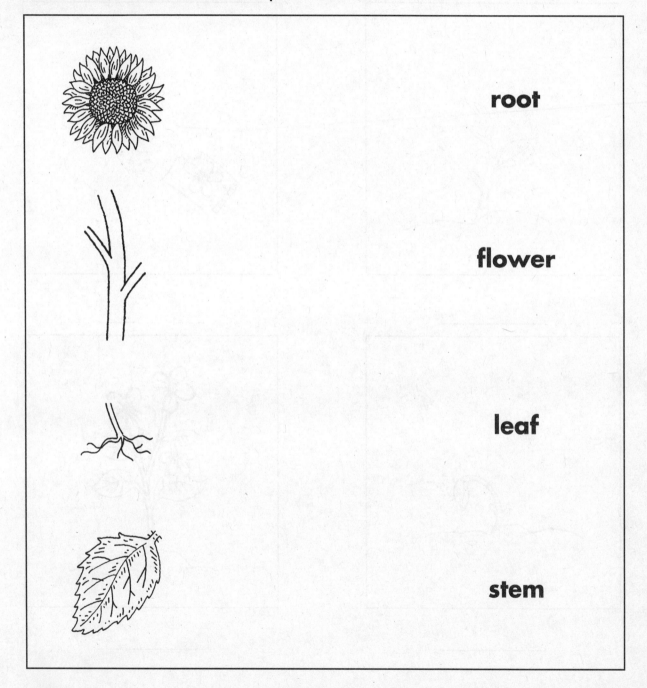

root

flower

leaf

stem

Directions: Name the plant parts on the left and the words for the parts on the right. Draw a line from each plant part to the word that names the plant part.
Home Activity: Show your child pictures of plants. Point to a flower, stem, leaf, or root and have your child name the part of the plant.

How do plants grow?

Show how a plant grows.
Number the pictures in order.

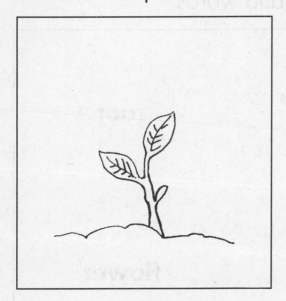

_____

_____

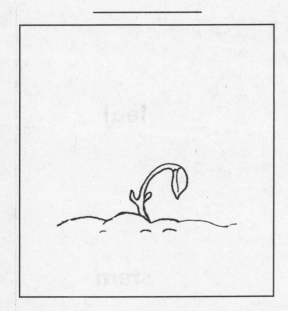

_____

_____

Directions: Tell what you see in each picture. Decide what is the correct order for the pictures. Write 1, 2, 3, or 4 on the line under each picture.
Home Activity: Find pictures of a baby, a child, a teenager, and an adult. Mix the pictures and ask your child to put the pictures in the correct order.

Dear Family,

In the science chapter Growing and Changing, your child is learning how living things change and grow. The class learned that baby animals grow into adult animals. The children also looked at the different ways animals move. The children also learned about the parts of a plant, and how a plant grows from a seed.

While learning about how living things grow and change, the children also learned many new vocabulary words. Help your child to make these words a part of his or her own vocabulary by using them when you talk together about how plants and animals grow and change.

grow
change
move
swim
alike
different
seed
tree
flowers
leaves

The following pages include activities that you and your child can do together. By participating in your child's education, you will help to bring the learning home.

Family Science Activity
Investigating Plants

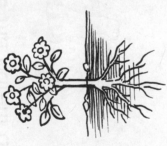

Steps

1. Take a walk inside your home and look at the houseplants with your child. You may also walk around your community and look at outdoor plants.

2. Help your child identify and say the parts of the plant: flower, leaf, and stem. Point out that the roots of a plant grow under the ground.

3. Encourage your child to draw a picture of one of the plants. Your child may also label the parts of the plant.

4. Display the picture in a central area.

5. If possible, you may show your child seeds such as acorns or sunflower seeds. Explain that a seed can grow into a plant.

Growing and Changing

A chicken begins life as an egg.
How does the egg change?
How does the egg become a chicken?

Draw 2 pictures that show what happens after an egg hatches.

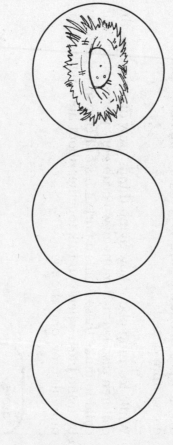

Fun Fact

After a chicken lays an egg, it takes about 21 days for it to hatch into a baby chick. Not all chicks are yellow. The color of a chick depends on what color its parents are.

Growing Up

Color the baby animals.
Circle the parent animals.

Picture Clues

Which animals live on land?
Draw lines from the animals to *Land*.
Which animals live in water?
Draw lines from the animals to *Water*.

Land

Water

 Directions: Name each animal and tell whether it lives on land or in water. In the first row, draw a line from the animal to the *Land* box if the animal lives on land. In the second row, draw a line from the animal to the *Water* box if the animal lives in water.

Home Activity: Show pictures of a dolphin, a rhinoceros, a porcupine, and a manatee. Ask your child whether each animal lives on land or in water. Have your child explain how he or she knew.

What are some plants and animals that live on land?

Draw a plant that lives on land.
Draw an animal that lives on land.

Plant and Animal That Live on Land

Directions: Think about animals and plants you know that live on land. Choose one animal and one plant and draw pictures of them in the box.
Home Activity: With your child, make a list of as many animals and plants that live on land as you can think of. Save the list.

What are some plants and animals that live in water?

Draw a plant that lives in water.
Draw an animal that lives in water.

Plant and Animal That Live in Water

Directions: Think about animals and plants you know that live in water. Choose one animal and one plant and draw pictures of them in the box.
Home Activity: With your child, make a list of as many animals and plants that live in water as you can think of. Compare this list to the one you made of animals and plants that live on land.

What are some plants and animals that live in hot places?

Color the picture that shows things living in a hot place.

Directions: Tell what you see in each picture. Look for clues that tell you whether or not the picture shows a hot place. Then color the picture that shows animals and plants living in a hot place.

Home Activity: Read your child a book about deserts. Talk about the kinds of animals and plants that live in the desert and how they are able to live there.

Name _____

What are some plants and animals that live in cold places?

Circle the animals that live in cold places.

Directions: Name each animal and tell whether or not it lives in a cold place. If you decide that it lives in a cold place, circle the picture of the animal. Explain how you decided.

Home Activity: Read your child a book about the Arctic. Talk about the kinds of animals and plants that live in the Arctic and how they are able to live there.

© Pearson Education, Inc.

What are some other places plants and animals live?

Where do the animals live?
Draw lines to match the animals and
their homes.

 Directions: Name the animals on the left and the places they live on the right.
Think about which animal lives in which place. Draw a line from each animal
to its home.
Home Activity: Name an animal and ask your child where the animal lives.
Then have your child name an animal and you tell where the animal lives.

Dear Family,

In the science chapter Plants and Animals All Around, your child learned about different kinds of places where animals live. The class explored ecosystems on land and in water. While exploring different habitats, the children learned about types of animals that live in each environment.

While learning about habitats, the children also learned many new vocabulary words. Help your child to make these words a part of his or her own vocabulary by using them when you talk together about habitats.

land
field
pond
ocean
desert
cactus
cold
snow
mountain
grassland

The following pages include activities that you and your child can do together. By participating in your child's education, you will help to bring the learning home.

Family Science Activity

Animal Habitat
Coloring Book

Materials
- magazines with animal pictures (optional)
- scissors
- glue (optional)
- paper
- crayons

Steps

1. Invite your child to make a coloring book with animals and habitats.

2. Fold two pieces of paper length-wise to make a book. You may also use construction paper to make a book cover.

3. Help your child draw pictures of animals. You may also cut out pictures of animals from magazines and glue them in the book.

4. Discuss with your child where each animal lives. Does it live in a forest, wetland, ocean, or desert?

5. Encourage your child to color in features of the animals' habitats, such as trees and plants.

6. Display the book in a central area.

Fun Fact

A dolphin breathes through a blowhole on top of its head. As the dolphin breathes, the air leaves the blowhole faster than 100 miles per hour. This is faster than a car on a highway!

Where Do Animals Live?

Look at the pictures of places on the left and animals on the right. **Draw** a line to match each place to an animal that lives there. **Color** the pictures.

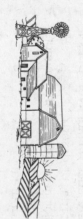

Counting

Count how many. Write the number.

_____

Directions: Count the things in each box. Write the number on the line.
Home Activity: Place groups of 1, 2, 3, and 4 pennies on a table. Have your child count the coins in each group, write the number on a scrap of paper, and label the group with the number.

Predict

Look at the picture.
Draw what you think will happen next.

I know.	I predict.

Directions: Look at the picture and tell what you see. Think about what the people might do next. Draw a picture showing what you think they will do.
Home Activity: Take an ice cube and put it in a dish. Ask your child what he or she thinks will happen next. Set up other similar situations and ask your child to predict.

Workbook

What makes up Earth's surface?

Color the things that are part of Earth's land.

Directions: Name each picture. Think about whether that object is part of Earth's land. Remember what you learned. Color the pictures that show parts of Earth's land.

Home Activity: Go for a walk with your child and look for soil, sand, pebbles, and rocks. Talk with your child about how these things make up Earth's land.

What are some of Earth's landforms?

Draw each kind of landform.

mountain

valley

plain

Directions: Review what a mountain, a valley, and a plain look like. Then draw pictures of these three landforms, one picture in each box.

Home Activity: Look through magazines with your child. Have your child find pictures of mountains, valleys, and plains. Ask your child to describe the pictures.

How can we use land on Earth?

Circle the pictures that show ways we use land.

 Directions: Look at each picture and tell what the person is doing. Think about whether the person is using Earth's land. Circle the picture if it shows a way that we use land.

Home Activity: Write *farming*, *logging*, *building*, and *gardening* on paper. Talk with your child about how these activities use Earth's land. Think of other activities to add to the list.

© Pearson Education, Inc.

Where is water found on Earth?

Where would you find water?
Color the places blue.

 Directions: Look at the scene and point out the four places where you would expect to find water. Color those places blue.

Home Activity: Write *pond, stream, river,* and *lake* on separate index cards. Read each word aloud and have your child place the card on the part of the scene the word names.

How do we use water and air?

Color the pictures that show ways we use water and air.

Directions: Describe what you see in each picture. Think about whether the picture shows a use of Earth's water or air. Color the picture if it shows a way that we use water or air.

Home Activity: Write *drinking* and *bathing* under *Water* and *blowing up balloons* and *keeping cool* under *Air*. Talk with your child about how these activities use Earth's water or air. Think of other activities to add to the lists.

How can you help care for Earth?

Circle the pictures that show ways we can help protect Earth.

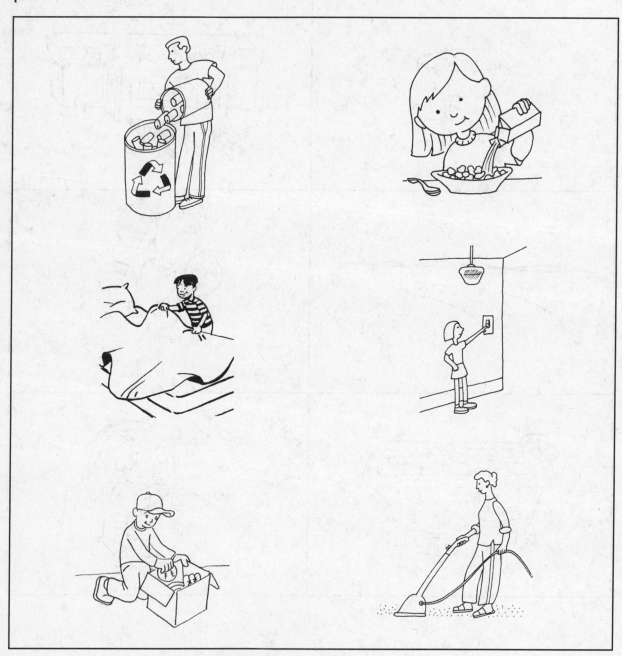

 Directions: Look at each picture and identify what the person is doing. Think about whether or not what the person is doing helps protect Earth. Circle the picture if it shows a way that we can help protect Earth.

Home Activity: Talk with your child about things you do at home that help protect Earth. Make a list. Then talk about things you could start doing.

Dear Family,

In the science chapter Our Land, Water, and Air, your child learned about different kinds of land and water. The class looked at Earth's landforms, such as valleys and mountains. They learned about water in oceans, lakes, and rivers. The class talked about how we use land, water, and air. While learning about Earth's resources, we also talked about recycling materials to help protect Earth.

While learning about Earth's land, water, and air, the children also learned many new vocabulary words. Help your child to make these words a part of his or her own vocabulary by using them when you talk together about land, water, and air.

Earth	lake	
rock	ice	windmill
shape		clearing
form		protect
farming		recycle
wood		
river		

The following pages include activities that you and your child can do together. By participating in your child's education, you will help to bring the learning home.

Family Science Activity
Set up a Recycling Center

Materials
- paper
- crayons
- tape
- large cardboard boxes or plastic totes

Steps

1. Talk with your child about recycling. Explain that when we recycle, we make new things out of used materials. For example, we can recycle used cans to make new cans.

2. Make labels for recycling containers. Write the names of materials that can be recycled in your community, such as "metal" or "glass." Use a separate sheet of paper for each material. Ask your child to draw a picture on each label, such as a bottle for the "glass" label or a can for the "metal" label.

3. Help your child tape the labels to the cardboard boxes or plastic totes.

4. Look for materials that can be recycled and help your child to identify the material. For example, is it glass, metal, plastic, or paper?

5. Encourage your child to think of any ways to reuse materials in the house and reduce the amount of trash.

6. If your neighborhood recycles materials, bring the materials to the recycling center with your child.

Color Earth

Find the rocks, sand and water.

Color the rocks gray. Color the sand brown. Color the water blue.

Fun Fact

Most of Earth is covered by water. Most of the water on Earth is salt water. Most of our body is made of water, too. We cannot live more than a week without drinking water.

Fun on Land and Water

Look at the pictures of places on the left.

How do we use land and water?

Draw a line to match the place to something you can do there.

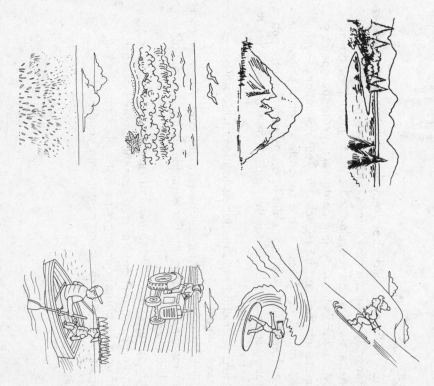

🎯 Put Things in Order

Put the pictures in order.
Write 1, 2, or 3.

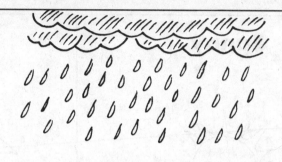

_____

_____

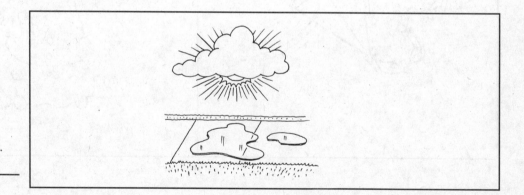

_____

Directions: Describe what you see in each picture. Think about which picture shows what comes first, next, or last. Write 1, 2, or 3 on the lines in front of each picture.
Home Activity: On separate sheets of paper, draw a leaf on a tree branch, a leaf falling, and a leaf on the ground. Ask your child to put the pictures into the correct order.

Name _____

What are different kinds of weather?

Look outside.
Color the picture that shows the weather today.

Sunny 	**Rainy** 
Windy 	**Snowy** 

Directions: Look out a window or go outside. What is the weather like today?
Choose the picture that looks most like the weather today. Color the picture.
Home Activity: Find a local weather report and map in a newspaper or on the
Internet. Talk about them with your child, including the symbols used and what
they stand for.

Name _____

What is spring?

Circle the things you might see on a spring day.

Directions: Tell what is happening in each picture. Think about whether this event could happen in the spring. Circle the picture if it shows something that might happen in the spring.

Home Activity: Using a large sheet of drawing paper and crayons or markers, draw a spring scene with your child. Talk about why you included the things you did in the picture.

Name _____

What is summer?

Color the picture that shows a summer day.

 Directions: Look at each scene and describe what you see. Think about what season each scene shows. Choose the picture that shows summer and color it.
Home Activity: With your child, make a list of activities that you like to do in the summer. Put a star by those activities that you can do only in the summer.

Name _____

What is fall?

Put an X on the thing you would <u>not</u> see on a fall day.

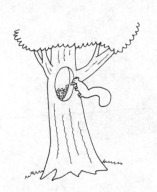

Directions: Look at the two pictures in each row. Decide which picture shows something that you would <u>not</u> see in the fall. Put a large X on that picture.
Home Activity: Write *Fall* on paper. With your child, brainstorm words and phrases that come to mind when you hear the word *Fall* and write them on the paper.

What is winter?

Color the things you might see on a winter day.

Directions: Tell what is happening in each picture. Think about whether this event could happen in the winter. Circle the picture if it shows something that might happen on a winter day.

Home Activity: With your child, draw a winter scene on a large sheet of drawing paper. Take turns adding things to the picture and explaining why you included those things.

Name _____

What are different kinds of storms?

Draw one kind of storm.

 Directions: Think about different kinds of storms, such as thunderstorms, hurricanes, tornadoes, and blizzards. Choose one storm and draw a picture of it in the box.
Home Activity: Tell your child about any experiences you have had with storms. Talk with your child about storms either of you have seen on television or in movies.

© Pearson Education, Inc.

Notes

Dear Family,

In the science chapter Weather and Seasons, your child learned about how the weather and seasons change. The class learned that the weather can be sunny, windy, rainy, or snowy. They learned about changes that happen during spring, summer, fall, and winter. While learning about weather, they also talked about dangerous storms such as hurricanes and tornadoes.

In addition to learning about the weather and seasons, the children also learned many new vocabulary words. Help your child to make these words a part of his or her own vocabulary by using them when you talk together about the weather and seasons.

weather	fall	windy
warm		winter
cool	spring	snowy
	rainy	storm
	summer	thunder
	sunny	lightning

The following pages include activities that you and your child can do together. By participating in your child's education, you will help to bring the learning home.

Family Science Activity

Weather Poster

Materials:
- poster board or large sheet of paper
- crayons

Steps

1. Draw a calendar on poster board, making boxes large enough for your child to draw in.

2. Invite your child to look out the window. Ask your child to tell you if it is sunny, cloudy, rainy, or snowy. Is the temperature warm or cold?

3. Ask your child to make a drawing in the correct date box showing today's weather. For example, your child can draw the sun, clouds or raindrops, or a hat and scarf if it is cold. Encourage your child to be creative.

4. Ask your child to observe and record the weather for the rest of the week on the weather poster. Ask your child to explain the poster at the end of the week.

5. Display the poster in a central area.

What Season Is It?

How are the seasons different?

Draw on the picture to show a season.

Color the picture.

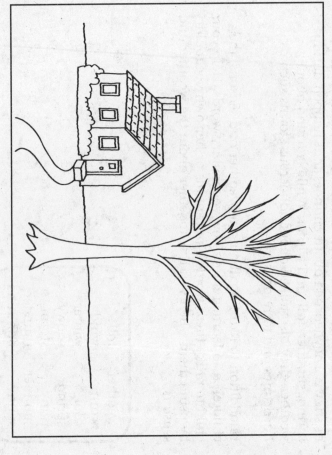

How Is the Weather?

Look at the pictures.

Color the Sun in the sunny day **yellow**.

Color the umbrella in the rainy day **red**.

Color the trees in the windy day **green**.

Color the boy's scarf in the snowy day **blue**.

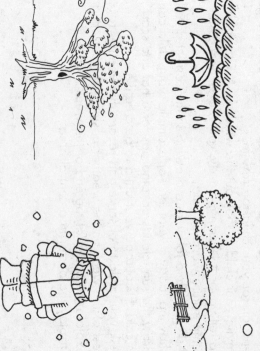

Adding

Count the groups.
Add the groups together.
Write the number.

+   =

_____

+   =

_____

+   =

_____

Directions: Count the objects in each group. Then add the numbers together.
Check by counting all the objects in both groups. Write the number on the lines.
Home Activity: Place two groups of beans or other small objects on a table and
ask your child to add the groups together. Continue with other groups.

Picture Clues

Which things are large?
Draw lines from the things to *Large*.
Which things can roll?
Draw lines from the things to *Can Roll*.

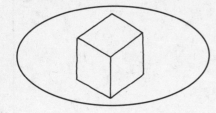 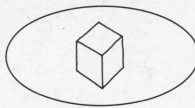 

Large

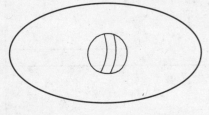 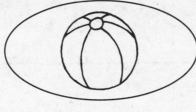 

Can Roll

Directions: Name each object. In the first row, draw a line from the object to the *Large* box if the object is large. In the second row, draw a line from the object to the *Can Roll* box if the object can roll.

Home Activity: Look around a room in your home. Have your child tell which things in the room are large, which are small, which can move, and which cannot move.

Use with pages 142–143.

What are some kinds of objects?

Circle the objects that are the same.

 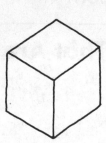

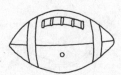 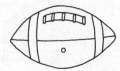

Directions: Look at the three pictures in each row. Decide which pictures show objects that are the same. Circle those pictures.

Home Activity: Place sets of three coins, two alike and one different, on a table. Have your child identify the coins that are the same.

What can you tell about objects?

Circle the things that are hard.
Circle the things that are soft.

Things That Are Hard

Things That Are Soft

Directions: Name the objects in the pictures. In the top box, circle the objects that are hard. In the bottom box, circle the objects that are soft.
Home Activity: Hold up an object, such as a stuffed toy or a vase. Ask your child to describe the object using as many different words as possible.

What is a solid?

Color the solids.

Directions: Look at the pictures. Which pictures show things that are solids? Remember that a solid has a shape. Choose the solids and color those pictures.
Home Activity: With your child, make a list of all the solids you find in one room of your home. Discuss how you know these things are solids.

Name _____

Name _____

Use with pages 148–149.

What is a liquid?

Circle the liquid in each row.

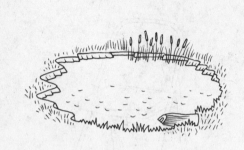   

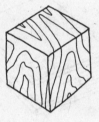   

Directions: Look at the two pictures in each row. Which picture shows something that is a liquid? Remember that a liquid takes the shape of what it is in. Choose the liquid and circle it.

Home Activity: Pour water into a glass. Ask your child which is a solid (glass) and which is a liquid (water) and have your child tell how he or she knew which was which.

Workbook

What is a gas?

Circle the things that have gas in them.

 Directions: Look at the pictures. Which pictures show things that have gases in them? Remember that a gas takes the shape of what it is in. Choose the things with gases and circle those pictures.

Home Activity: Blow up a balloon. Then let the air out so that your child can feel it. Blow up the balloon again. Ask your child which is a solid (balloon) and which is a gas (air) and have your child tell how he or she knew which was which.

Name _____

How can you change solids, liquids, and gases?

Circle the picture that shows how the thing in the first picture can change.

 Directions: Tell what you see in the first picture. Look at the other two pictures. Decide which picture shows how the ice cube can change. Circle that picture. Do the same with the sheet of paper and the loaf of bread.

Home Activity: Pour water into a glass cup. Discuss with your child what would happen to the water if you heated it and what would happen if you froze it.

© Pearson Education, Inc.

Dear Family,

In the science chapter Matter, your child explored how objects can be different sizes, shapes, colors, and weights. The class learned that matter can be a solid, liquid, or a gas. While learning about the different kinds of matter, the children also explored how matter can be changed. For example, liquids can be frozen into solid form.

In addition to learning about matter, the children learned many new vocabulary words. Help your child to make these words a part of his or her own vocabulary by using them when you talk together about matter.

size	liquid	
color	float	sink
weight	gas	
hard		container
soft	matter	fold
	solid	bend
freeze		

The following pages include activities that you and your child can do together. By participating in your child's education, you will help to bring the learning home.

© Pearson Education, Inc.

Family Science Activity

Homemade Popsicles

Materials:
- fruit juice or sweetened juice drink
- empty ice-cube tray
- toothpicks

Steps

1. Help your child learn how a liquid can be changed into a solid by making popsicle cubes in your kitchen.

2. First, talk to your child about solids. Ask your child to point out solid objects in the kitchen such as the refrigerator, kitchen counter, and the ice-cube tray. Then, talk about liquids, such as water, juice, and milk.

3. Place an empty ice cube tray on the counter. Pour juice into several sections. Place the tray in the freezer.

4. After the juice has partially frozen (about 1/2 hour), carefully insert toothpicks in the center of each cube. Ask your child to describe what is happening to the juice. (It is getting harder and starting to freeze.)

5. When the cubes are ready, invite your child to present them to the family and explain how the liquid juice is now a frozen solid.

Workbook

A Room Full of Toys

Color the picture.
Count the number of objects.

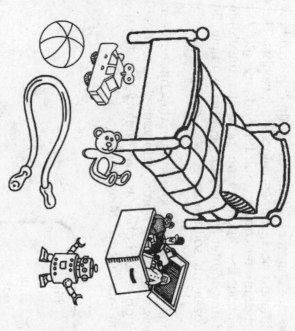

Talk About It

After the picture is colored, talk about it. How many objects are there? Toys, shoes, and books are all objects. What colors are they? Which ones are hard, soft, heavy, or light?

Solids, Liquids, and Gases

A solid has a shape.
Tables and chairs are solids.
A liquid can change shape.
Water is a liquid.
A gas can change shape and size.
Air is a gas. Air is in a balloon.

Look at the pictures. Color the solid **red**. Color the liquid **blue**. Color the gas **yellow**.

⦿ Predict

Look at the picture.
Draw what you think will happen next.

I Know   **I Predict**

→

Directions: Look at the picture and tell what you see. Think about what the boy might do next. Draw a picture showing what you think he will do.

Home Activity: Put a pot of water on the stove and turn on the burner. Ask your child what he or she thinks will happen next. Set up other similar situations and ask your child to predict.

What do you get from the Sun?

Draw a picture of something the Sun does.

Directions: How does the Sun help us? Think about what the Sun does. Draw a picture that shows one of the things the Sun does.

Home Activity: Draw a large Sun in the center of a sheet of paper. Around the Sun, help your child draw things that need the Sun.

How can you make a shadow?

Circle the things that have shadows.

 Directions: Look at the two pictures in each box. Circle the picture that shows something that has a shadow.
Home Activity: Hold a flashlight while your child uses his or her hands to make shadows on the wall. Then have your child hold the flashlight while you make shadows.

What gives off heat?

Color the things that give off heat.

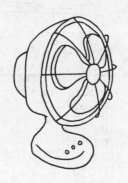

Directions: Look at the two pictures in each row. Decide which picture shows something that gives off heat. Color that picture.

Home Activity: Write *stove*, *fire*, and *Sun* on paper. With your child, try to think of other things that give off heat and add them to the list.

What makes these objects work?

Color the things that use energy.

 Directions: Look at the two pictures in each row. Decide which picture shows something that uses energy. Color that picture.
Home Activity: Write *Energy* on paper. With your child, brainstorm words and phrases that come to mind when you hear the word *Energy* and write them on the paper.

Notes

Dear Family,

In the science chapter Heat and Light, your child explored how we get heat and light from the Sun. The class learned that fire gives off heat. While learning about different kinds of heat and light, the children also explored how electricity helps make objects work.

In addition to learning about heat and light, the children learned many new vocabulary words. Help your child to make these words a part of his or her own vocabulary by using them when you talk together about heat and light.

Sun
heat
shadows
shade
stove
friction
energy
electricity

The following pages include activities that you and your child can do together. By participating in your child's education, you will help to bring the learning home.

Family Science Activity
Shadow Silhouettes

Materials:
- flashlight, lamp, or other source of light
- poster board or paper
- tape
- pencil

Steps

1. You can teach your child about shadows by creating shadows with a flashlight or a lamp.

2. Turn off all the lights in a room except for the flashlight or lamp. Have your child sit down sideways between the light and the wall. (Your child should not face the light.) This will cast a profile shadow, or silhouette.

3. Tape a piece of paper or poster board on the wall where your child's shadow falls.

4. Trace your child's shadow onto the paper.

5. Show your child his or her silhouette. Explain that this is the outline of your child's shadow on the wall.

6. Encourage your child to color his or her silhouette.

7. Display the finished silhouette in a central area.

Making a Shadow

Look at the girl. She is making a shadow. Color the Sun **yellow**. Color the shadow **a dark color**.

Talk About It!

Many things give off heat. The Sun gives heat. Rubbing your hands together makes heat. Rubbing your hands together makes heat. Rub your hands together and see if they get warm! What else makes heat?

What Gives Off Heat?

Look at the pictures. **Circle** the things that give off heat. **Color** the pictures.

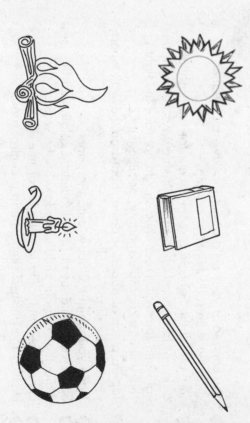

Put Things in Order

Put the pictures in order.
Write 1, 2, or 3.

_____

_____

_____

Directions: Describe what you see in each picture. Think about which picture shows what comes first, next, or last. Write 1, 2, or 3 on the lines in front of each picture.
Home Activity: On separate sheets of paper, draw a ball at the top of a ramp, the ball halfway down the ramp, and the ball on the ground at the bottom of the ramp. Mix the pictures. Ask your child to put the pictures into the correct order.

How can you use objects?

Circle the things you can push.
Circle the things you can pull.

push

pull

Directions: Look at the pictures in the top box. Circle the pictures that show things you can move by pushing. Look at the pictures in the bottom box. Circle the pictures that show things you can move by pulling.
Home Activity: Have your child use a toy wagon or a toy car and a piece of string to demonstrate the difference between pushing and pulling.

What are some ways objects move?

Color the things that can move.

  Directions: Name each object. Circle the picture if it shows something that is moving. Tell whether the object moves up and down, back and forth, or around and around.

Home Activity: With your child, look around your home and find things that move by going up and down, back and forth, or around and around.

How else can objects move?

Color the things that can move.

Directions: Look at the two pictures in each row. Decide which picture shows something that can move. Color that picture.

Home Activity: Show three things that can move to your child. Ask your child to tell and then demonstrate how the things move.

How fast can it move?

Circle the thing that moves fast.
Put an X on the thing that moves slow.

 Directions: Look at the two pictures in each box. Think about what moves fast and what moves slow. Circle the picture that shows something that moves fast. Put an X on the picture that shows something that moves slow.
Home Activity: Write *Fast* and *Slow* at the top of a sheet of paper. With your child, think of things to write under each word. Begin with the things on the page.

What does it sound like?

Color the things that make loud sounds.
Color the things that make soft sounds.

loud

soft

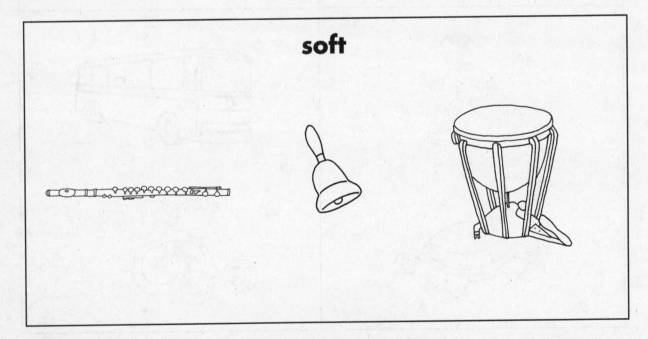

Directions: Name each animal or musical instrument. Think about the sounds that the animals and instruments make. In the top box, color the animals that make loud sounds. In the bottom box, color the instruments that make soft sounds.

Home Activity: Write *Loud* and *Soft* at the top of a sheet of paper. With your child, think of things to write under each word. Begin with the things on the page.

What do magnets do?

Draw something that the magnet can attract, or pull.

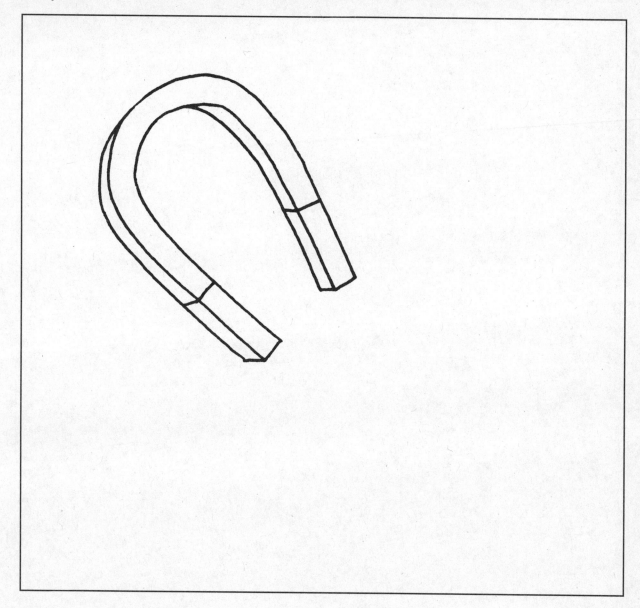

Directions: Think about things that magnets attract, or pull toward them. Draw a picture of something that a magnet will attract.

Home Activity: Let your child use a horseshoe magnet to test a variety of household objects to see which ones are attracted to the magnet. Ask your child how those objects are alike.

Notes

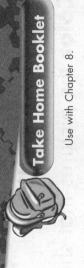

Dear Family,

In the science chapter How Things Move, your child learned that things can move up and down, around and around, and back and forth. The class learned that things like carts can be pushed or pulled. They explored how fast things can move, and what sounds certain objects make. Finally, they explored how magnets can push and pull objects.

In addition to learning about how things move, the children learned many new vocabulary words. Help your child to make these words a part of his or her own vocabulary by using them when you talk together about how things move.

pushing	fast
pulling	slow
direction	sound
places	loud
fly	magnet
turn	attract
twirl	metal

The following pages include activities that you and your child can do together. By participating in your child's education, you will help to bring the learning home.

Family Science Activity

Fun with Magnets!

Materials:

- magnet
- small metal objects, such as paper clips, keys, batteries, nails, pins, and lids of jars
- nonmetal objects made of glass, plastic, paper, or other materials
- paper
- crayons

Steps

1. Show your child a magnet. Talk about how magnets push and pull some things.

2. Set out several small metal objects, such as keys, paper clips, or batteries. Have your child try the magnet on each object. Does it push or pull the objects?

3. Now, set out several plastic or glass objects, such as a cup or bowl. Ask your child to try the magnet on these objects. Ask your child to tell you which objects the magnet does not seem to attract.

4. Invite your child to make a drawing of objects that are affected by the magnet. Ask him or her to name the objects and tell what happened with the magnet.

5. Ask your child to show the drawing to the family. Display it in a central area.

Push or Pull?

Color the pictures that show something you pull.
Circle the pictures that show something you push.

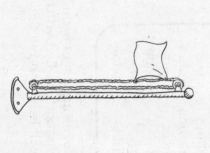

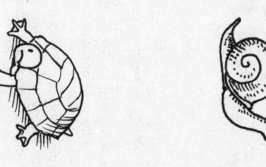

How Fast Is It?

Color the fast things **red**.
Color the slow things **blue**.

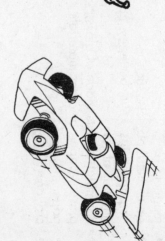

Workbook

Patterns

Look at the pattern.
Draw what comes next.

Directions: Name the shapes in the first row. Think about the pattern of the shapes. Draw the shape that comes next in the pattern. Do the same with the second and third rows.

Home Activity: Make a penny-penny-nickel pattern on a table. Offer pennies, nickels, and dimes and ask your child to use the coins to continue the pattern. Then make other patterns with the coins.

Alike and Different

How are the night sky and the day sky alike?
Draw a day sky and a night sky.
Show how they are different.

Alike	Different

 Directions: Look at the pictures in the left box. Tell how the day sky and the night sky are alike. Then draw pictures of the day sky and the night sky that show how they are different.

Home Activity: Show your child pairs of household objects, such as a fork and a knife, and ask your child how the objects are alike and different. (Both are used for eating; the fork is used to pick up food, while the knife is used for cutting food.)

What can you see in the daytime sky?

Circle the things you can see in the sky during the day.

Directions: Name the pictures. Circle the pictures that show things you can see in the sky during the day.

Home Activity: With your child, draw a daytime scene that also shows the day sky. Talk about what you both want to include in the picture and why these things are appropriate for a daytime picture.

What can you see in the nighttime sky?

Circle the things you can see in the sky at night.

 Directions: Name the pictures. Circle the pictures that show things you can see in the sky at night.
Home Activity: With your child, draw a nighttime scene that also shows the night sky. Talk about what you both want to include in the picture and why these things are appropriate for a nighttime picture.

How does the sky change during the day?

Show what happens first, next, and last.
Write 1, 2, or 3.

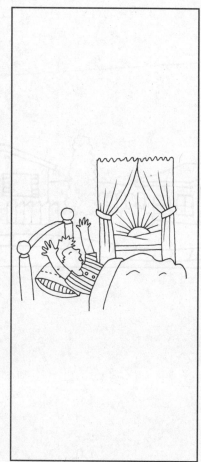

_____   _____   _____

Directions: Describe what you see in each picture. Think about which picture shows what comes first, next, or last. Write 1, 2, or 3 on the lines under each picture.

Home Activity: Cut a large circle from yellow construction paper. Talk with your child about what time it is as you hold the "Sun" overhead in different locations.

How does the Moon change?

Draw a full Moon.
Draw a crescent Moon.

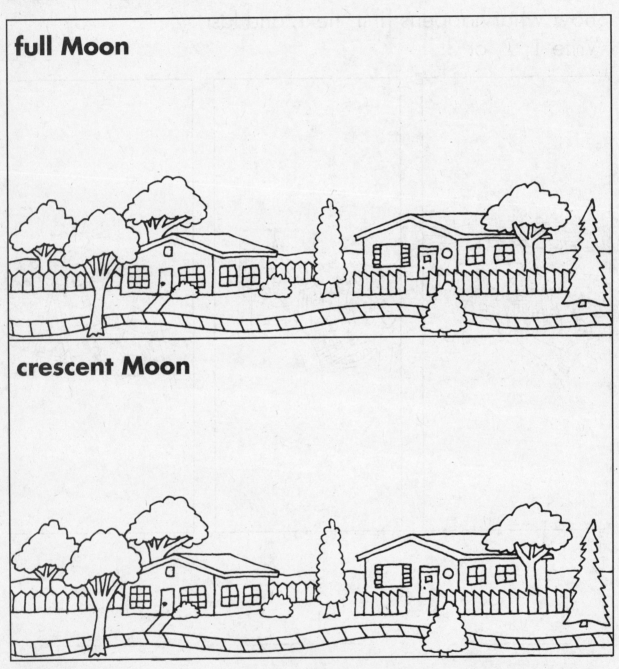

full Moon

crescent Moon

Directions: Think about how a full Moon looks. Draw a full Moon in the top box. Think about how a crescent Moon looks. Draw a crescent Moon in the bottom box.

Home Activity: Cut one large circle from white paper and one large circle from black paper. With your child, place the black circle over the white circle to show the different phases of the Moon.

© Pearson Education, Inc.

Workbook

Dear Family,

In the science chapter Day and Night, your child learned how day and night are alike and different. The class learned about clouds, stars, the Sun, and the Moon. They talked about how the sky changes during the day and night. The class also talked about how the Moon changes every night.

In addition to learning about day and night, the children learned many new vocabulary words. Help your child to make these words a part of his or her own vocabulary by using them when you talk together about day and night.

day
sky
cloud
night
Moon
stars
rise
set
morning
evening
full Moon
new Moon

The following pages include activities that you and your child can do together. By participating in your child's education, you will help to bring the learning home.

Family Science Activity
The Moon Matching Game

Materials:
- cardboard or construction paper
- crayons or markers
- scissors

Steps

1. Play a matching game with phases of the Moon. Cut cardboard or construction paper into eight equal-sized rectangles.

2. Give your child two of the rectangles and ask him or her to draw a full Moon on both.

3. Create a pair of "cards" for a half Moon and a crescent Moon.

4. Leave two of the cards blank. Explain that this is the new Moon.

5. Turn the cards face-down on a table or flat surface.

6. Take turns turning over two cards and trying to get a matching pair. If a player gets a matching pair, he or she must say what phase of the Moon the pair is. The player keeps the pair.

7. Keep playing until all cards have been matched. Whoever has the most pairs is the winner.

How Does the Moon Change?

The Moon changes a little every night.

Color the full Moon yellow.

Color the half Moon orange.

Talk About It

After the picture is colored, talk about it. Does the Moon always look the same? How does it change? What shape is the Moon when it is full? Explain that we can't see the Moon at all when there is a new Moon.

What's in the Sky?

How does the sky look during the day?

How does it look at night?

Draw what you find in the sky—during the day and at night.

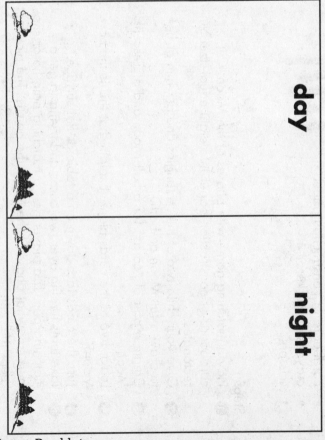

day	night

Workbook

Name _____

Picture Clues

Which machines help us go places?
Draw lines from the machines to *Go Places.*
Which machines help us do work?
Draw lines from the machines to *Do Work.*

   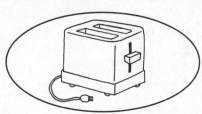   

Go Places

   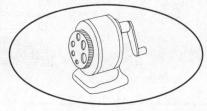   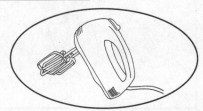

Do Work

 Directions: In the first row, draw a line from the machine to the *Go Places* box if the machine helps us go places. In the second row, draw a line from the machine to the *Do Work* box if the machine helps us do work.

Home Activity: Write *Go Places* and *Do Work* on a sheet of paper. Ask your child to think of machines that help us go places or do work. Begin with the machines on the page. Write the machines under the phrases. (Some machines can be put under both.)

Name _____

What are some simple machines?

Circle the simple machine.

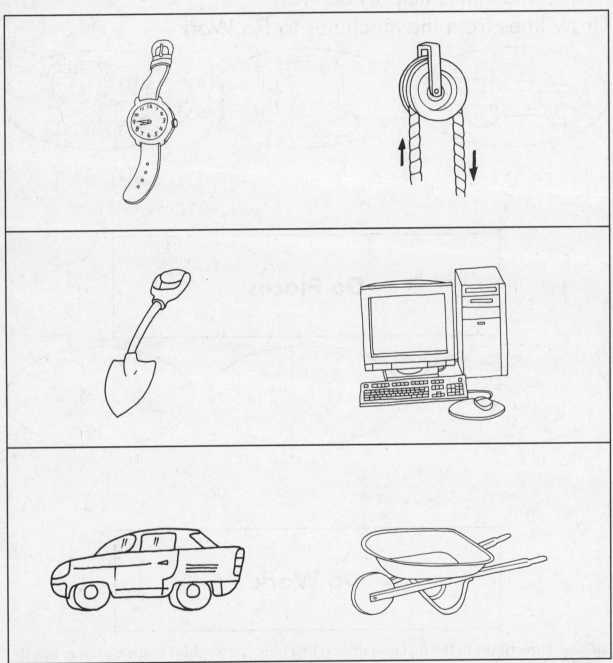

Directions: Look at the two pictures in each row. Name the machines in the pictures. Circle the picture that shows a simple machine.

Home Activity: With your child, find one example of a wheel, a pulley, a lever, and a ramp in your home. Talk about how each simple machine makes work easier.

Workbook

What are some other kinds of machines?

Color the machine.

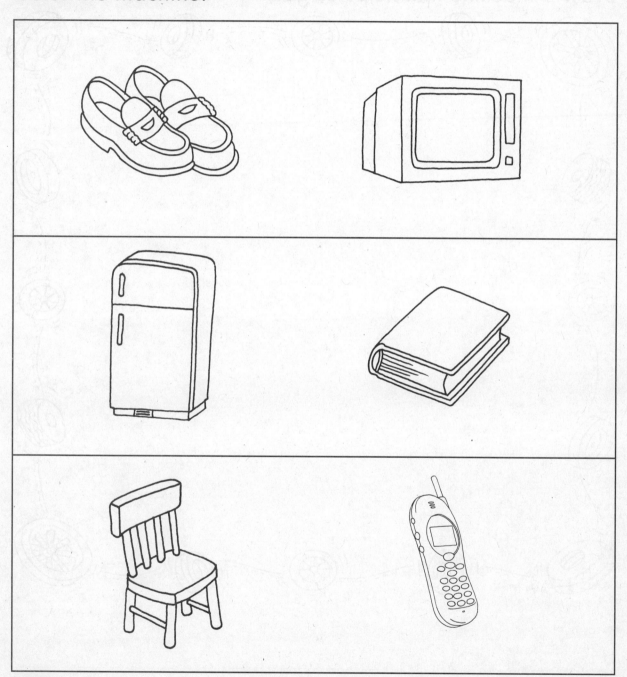

Directions: Look at the two pictures in each row. Name the pictures. Think about which picture shows a common machine. Color that picture.

Home Activity: With your child, make a list of common machines that you have in your home. Begin with the machines on the page. (Remember, a machine does not always use electricity or batteries.)

Name _____

What machines help us move from place to place?

Draw a machine that helps us go.

 Directions: Think about machines that help people get from one place to another. Draw a picture of one of these machines. Label it if you can.

Home Activity: Act out a machine that people use to get around. Have your child guess what machine you are acting out. Then let your child act out a machine while you guess.

Name _____

Why do we use machines?

Circle the machine that helps us do our work.

Directions: Look at the two pictures in each box. Decide which picture shows a machine that helps us do our work. Circle that picture.

Home Activity: Take turns with your child naming machines that help us do work. Begin with the machines on the page. Continue until neither of you can think of any more appropriate machines.

© Pearson Education, Inc.

How does a bicycle work?

Circle the parts of a bike.

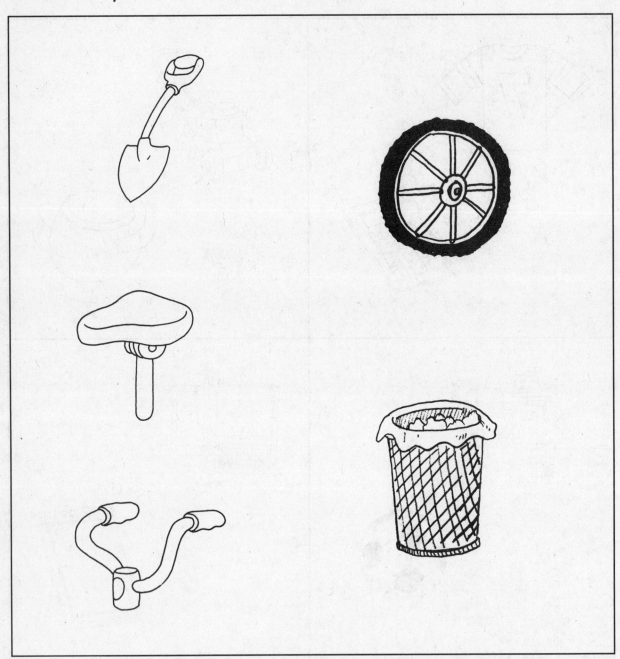

 Directions: Name the pictures. Think about which pictures show parts that help make a bicycle work. Circle the pictures of the bicycle parts.
Home Activity: Find a machine that has only a few parts, such as a pair of scissors. Talk with your child about the parts and how the parts work together to make the machine work.

© Pearson Education, Inc.

Dear Family,

Your child is learning about machines. In the science chapter How Things Work, the class learned about some simple machines such as wheels, levers, pulleys, and ramps. The class learned that machines help us do our work, move things, and travel from place to place.

In addition to learning about machines, the children learned many new vocabulary words. Help your child to make these words a part of his or her own vocabulary by using them when you talk together about how we use machines.

simple machine	plane
wheel	train
lever	car
pulley	invent
ramp	invention
computer	work
lamp	bicycle
bus	part

The following pages include activities that you and your child can do together. By participating in your child's education, you will help to bring the learning home.

Family Science Activity

Machines in Magazines

Materials:
- magazines
- glue
- scissors
- poster board

Steps

1. Look at magazines together with your child. Ask your child to point out any machines in the magazines.
2. Help your child to cut out the pictures of machines as he or she names them.
3. Assemble the pictures and help your child paste them in a collage on the poster board. Allow the collage to dry.
4. Encourage your child to point to each picture, name it, and tell what each machine does.
5. Display the collage in a central area of the house.

Workbook

Simple Machines

Look at the things on the left.
Look at the machines on the right.
Draw a line to match something on the left to a machine that can help you use it. **Color** the pictures.

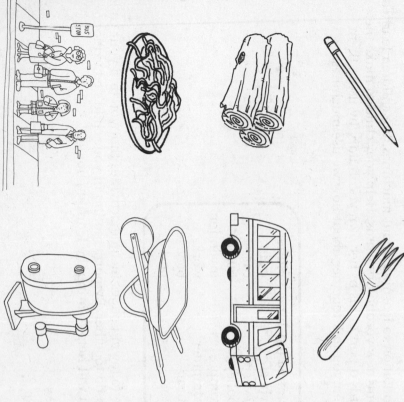

Machines in Our Lives

Look for machines in the picture.
Color the machines with a blue crayon.

Picture Graphs

Each 😊 stands for one child.
Count the children in each row.
Color the machine that has the most children.

How Do You Get to School?	
🚌	😊 😊
🚗	😊 😊 😊 😊
🚆	😊 😊
🚲	😊 😊 😊

Directions: Count the faces to find out how many children go to school on or in each kind of machine. Color the machine that the largest number of children use to get to school.

Home Activity: Ask your child questions about the picture graph, such as *How many more children go to school in a car than on a bus?* (2) *Which do more children use to get to school—a train or a bicycle?* (bicycle)

Notes